MW01194391

Learning to Breathe:
Mastering the Art of Spiritual Respiration

Chris Lohrstorfer

Learning to Breathe

Mastering the Art of Spiritual Respiration

CHRIS LOHRSTORFER

TELEIOS PRESS

Copyright © 2018 Teleios Press
Jackson, MS

TeleiosPress.com

All rights reserved, unless otherwise stated in the text. No part
of this book may be reproduced or transmitted in any form or
by any means, electronic or mechanical, including photocopy-
ing, recording, or by any information storage or retrieval system,
without permission in writing from the Publisher.

Printed in the United States of America

First edition 2018

All scripture references taken from
The Holman Christian Standard Translation

Copyright © Holman Bible Publishers

All references to the Works of John Wesley are taken from an
online source at www.wesley.nnu.edu

Cover design by Two Cups Creative

I have been blessed to have many
inspiring students over the years – this is for them.

CONTENTS

INTRODUCTION

I love being a teacher. Over the years I have been privileged to train and shape the minds of students who have spread out over the planet to continue the process in the lives of others.

What I love is, sometimes in the middle of a lecture, when the light goes on, the realization strikes – and the potential of the life of God in us becomes a reality to the student.

I love this because your relationship with God is the most important, as well as the most elusive, relationship you will have in your life.

Relationship with God is to your soul what breathing is to your lungs. But how can humans— made of the dust of the earth and physically and temporally limited—know the Eternal and Unchanging God of the Universe? He is Spirit; we are flesh. We are located in time and space in a mortal body; He is unlimited in all things. It seems impossible that we would be able to be intimate with Him.

That's what this book is all about.

What I propose to you in these pages is a relationship with God based on His relational nature, best described as "shared life." God gives us His life, and we offer it back to Him in worship and praise. Breathe in His grace; breathe out His grace. This interaction with the life of God is called Spiritual Respiration.

I learned of the process of Spiritual Respiration from my time studying the eighteenth-century English preacher and theologian, John Wesley. Best known as the father of Methodism, Wesley was the heart, soul, and mind behind the Wesleyan Revival that spread across England, Europe, and into the United States.

Wesley spent his days traveling, preaching, and starting groups for discipleship. Why did he do it? Because the pastors around him were not "caring for the souls of men." This was his calling, his passion: to help all those who would "flee the wrath to come," become all that God intended for them to become. And he did it through organizing them together for mutual growth and strength. In this way, he gave their souls "time and means to grow."

In his sermon entitled *The Great Privilege of those That are Born of God*, John Wesley described Spiritual Respiration as an "immediate inspiration" of God's Spirit into the soul of the believer. The process of receiving that breath and offering it back to God is how the Christian's spiritual relationship with God works. It takes both God's action and our reaction to it. Wesley wrote,

> *The Spirit or breath of God is immediately inspired, breathed into the new-born soul; and the same breath which comes from, returns to, God: As it is continually received by faith, so it is continually rendered back by love, by prayer, and praise, and thanksgiving; love and praise, and prayer being the breath of every soul which is truly born of God. And by this new kind of spiritual respiration, spiritual life is not only sustained, but increased day by day, together with spiritual*

strength, and motion, and sensation; all the senses of the soul being now awake, and capable of discerning spiritual good and evil.

Now one who is so born of God, as hath been above described, who continually receives into his soul the breath of life from God, the gracious influence of his Spirit, and continually renders it back; one who thus believes and loves, who by faith perceives the continual actings of God upon his spirit, and by a kind of spiritual re-action returns the grace he receives, in unceasing love, and praise, and prayer.

Relationship with God is just that simple: He acts, we react. He gives us grace—His life—and we receive it and then offer ourselves back to God. The Apostle Paul described it this way:

Therefore, brothers, by the mercies of God, I urge you to present your bodies as a living sacrifice, holy and pleasing to God; this is your spiritual worship.[1]

This is the essence of discipleship. This is the basis of spiritual life. This is what it means to have a relationship with God that is intimate, personal, and active.

One of the focal points of salvation is transformation. The Bible calls it sanctification—the transformation of our nature by the grace of God. But, I want to be clear here: Transformation occurs through a personal relationship with God. It is His presence in us that allows the fruit of the Spirit (the reproduction of the Spirit's nature into our own) to occur.

You cannot expect holiness without relationship.

Salvation is more than a legal overlooking of your faults. I think we do a grave disservice to Christians when we proclaim a gospel that is only based on forgiveness.

Christianity is not just a legal action—it is a life-changing, nature-rearranging, hope-giving relationship. God has much more for you, but it will only come through a vital, living relationship with the living God. That is why knowing how to walk with God is so important.

Life comes through His grace. What we need to know is how to receive it—how to breathe in God's grace. Does He have specific actions or means through which this can take place?

We also need to know how to breathe it back again. How can I re-act to His actions in me? What can I do daily to ensure that I am actively engaged in Spiritual Respiration?

In Chapters One and Two we will address the need for, possibility of, and process used for relationship with the Divine Being. In Chapter Three we will see the means of breathing in God's grace and in Chapter Four the means of breathing out His grace. We will finish with a discussion of the importance of making this process a lifelong practice in Chapter Five. Because this spiritual life is not meant to be lived alone, I have included in the Appendix a guide for a group discussion.

Special Thanks

I appreciate all who have helped me think through this process of shared life—the instructors over the years who have inspired a heart-level search in me; students who have questioned everything; my fellow pilgrims who, along the way have sometimes pulled me, sometimes pushed me; and my Church family who have challenged me to share life with them every day. I also thank those who have pushed me to write; they may eventually regret it. Thanks to Matt Friedeman, Mary Friedeman, and David Phillips of Teleios Press, and my friend and editor Melissa Woods.

CHAPTER ONE

The Great Privilege

For through Him we both have access by one Spirit to the Father.[1]

How often have we heard Christians proclaim that Christianity is "not just a religion, it's a relationship?" What do you suppose they mean by that? When you ask about it they will usually describe it something like this: "God has forgiven my sins, and now I try to live for Him, and I look forward to when I can go to heaven and meet Him face to face."

I have to be honest with you, that sounds more like an arranged marriage than a real, present-tense, intimate relationship. This may explain the conundrum that the Church often finds itself in—we believe in a living God but we don't experience Him much.

Shared life is the basis of the very nature of God.

Here is the irony: this lack of experiencing God is the difference between religion and relationship.

That means the same people who proclaim the relationship are often the ones who best live out the definition of the religion.

Perhaps the best biblical picture we have of our potential relationship to God is found in the Greek word *koinonia*. *Koinonia* has at its core koinos, which means "common." The concept of *koinonia* is about communion, shared life. It is often translated as fellowship.

Shared life is the basis of the very nature of God. Before anything was created, in eternity past when God simply was, He was shared life. The Father was begetting the Son, as the Spirit communicated the very substance of the Father in a relationship of life and love.

This is what we call Trinitarian Relationship. It defines God for us: He is a loving Father who shares His life with others— eternally in the Son, but also with mankind in the life-giving breath He breathed into Adam.

> *Then the Lord God formed the man out of the dust from the ground and breathed the breath of life into his nostrils, and the man became a living being.*[2]

What is that breath of life so freely given to Adam? The Hebrew word *neshamah*, used in Genesis 2, is translated as "breath, life, or inspiration." The breath of God, breathed into the very soul of Adam is not something unusual; it is reflective of the nature of God. In fact, it is a reflection of the very relationship that we call God. He gives Himself to others, and He made us to know Him intimately. This is the primary reason for making us in His image.

Remember, knowing something about God is not the same thing as knowing God. That's why, when Jesus talked about eternal life, He used a relational term for knowledge.

> *This is eternal life: that they may know You, the only true God, and the One You have sent—Jesus Christ.*[3]

The word "know" in this verse is interesting. This is not "knowledge about" God. To "know God" would mean you are intimate with Him.

Some people might ask – "Is it possible for us to know Him?" The answer to that is a resounding "YES!" And here's why we can know Him—first, because the Father made us to know Him.

In the early fourth century, Athanasius of Alexandria wrote a definitive work called *On the Incarnation of the Word*, which became foundational for Trinitarian theology for the whole of the Church. In Chapter One, in his discussion of our origin he said,

> *Upon them, therefore... He bestowed a grace which other creatures lacked—namely the impress of His own Image, a share in the reasonable being of the very Word Himself, so that, reflecting Him... they might continue forever in the blessed and only true life of the saints in paradise.*[4]

He bestowed a grace—that's the first part of the Great Privilege. God Himself gave us something which we could not have otherwise. He infused us at creation with His very image; He made us like Him. And why? Because, as Athanasius tells us, we were created to reflect the Son—the Son begotten by the love of the Father through the Spirit's infusion; the Son relating, loving, sharing life with the Father.

That's whom we were made to be like: created beings "reflecting Him" with a "share in the reasonable being of the very Word Himself."

In Revelation 4, when praising God around His throne, the Elders say,

> *Our Lord and God, You are worthy to receive glory and honor and power, because You have created all things, and because of Your will they exist and were created.*[5]

Creation occurred just because God wanted to create. We exist for Him. But why? From John 3:16 we know that God loves us. Think of it—God made us because He wanted to, and what He felt toward us was love. He made us in His image, with the plan that we would be His children. We were made to be in a relationship with God.

We were created to reflect the Son – the Son begotten by the love of the Father through the Spirit's infusion; the Son relating, loving, sharing life with the Father.

That certainly is a great privilege.

Because we were made for relationship with the Divine Being, man's fall in Genesis 3 is a devastating turn of events. Imagine being given such a great privilege and then throwing it away for a piece of fruit.

It happened, and now we live with the consequences of it.

One of the issues we all struggle with is the one the Apostle Paul concludes in Romans chapter 3.

For all have sinned and fall short of the glory of God.[6]

The question we ask ourselves is this: "Having fallen from what God made us to be, is it still possible to know Him in an intimate relationship in this life?"

The second reason we can know Him is that the Son came to make a way for us to have that relationship.

Because of our need as sinners, God had to put a saving plan into place.[7] That plan was fulfilled in the sacrificial work of Jesus. Athanasius said,

> It was our sorry case that caused the Word to come down, our transgression that called out His love for us, so that He made haste to help us and to appear among us. It is we who were the cause of His taking human form, and for our salvation that in His great love He was both born and manifested in a human body.[8]

Our "sorry case" (as Athanasius put it) was the reason Jesus came. It is ironic that the One we were meant to reflect, reflected us. The Son of God became the Son of Man, so that the sons of men can become the sons of God. In becoming the sons of God, we become something which God had always intended for us.

In reflecting us, Jesus brought us into relationship with God the Father. In our self-imposed death, He offered us life. That life comes in knowing God, having an intimate relationship with Him.

In John's gospel, John tells us that when Jesus was coming to the end of His earthly life and was facing the cross, He entered into a private time of prayer—a prayer we call the High Priestly Prayer. [9]

The prayer begins like this:

> *Father, the hour has come. Glorify Your Son so that the Son may glorify You, for You gave Him authority over all flesh; so He may give eternal life to all You have given Him. This is eternal life: that they may know You, the only true God, and the One You have sent—Jesus Christ.* [10]

While it is a great privilege to have been created for relationship with God, it is even a greater privilege that the Son of God would give Himself as a sacrifice for us to be brought back to relationship with God.

The third reason we can know Him is because the Holy Spirit was sent to personally bring us into that relationship.

Relationship with God is not only possible, it has been provided by the love of God incarnate, the love of God in action, and the love of God infused in us by His presence.

Paul described the Spirit's work of drawing us into relationship with God as beginning with adoption. This is passive on our part—something He did for us. Our response is simply to receive the Spirit and the relationship He brings.

> *All those led by God's Spirit are God's sons. For you did not receive a spirit of slavery to fall back into fear, but you received the Spirit*

of adoption, by whom we cry out, "Abba, Father!"[11]

Relationship with God is not only possible, it has been provided by the love of God incarnate, the love of God in action, and the love of God infused in us by His presence through the Spirit.

Someone described God's redemption of us in this way: "The Father thought it, the Son bought it, and the Spirit brought it."

As the Apostle Paul said,

> *For through Him (Jesus) we both have access by one Spirit to the Father.[12]*

If you've been struggling with this great privilege, keep reading.

CHAPTER TWO

The Need to Breathe

And by this new kind of spiritual respiration, spiritual life is not only sustained, but increased day by day, together with spiritual strength, and motion, and sensation; all the senses of the soul being now awake, and capable of discerning spiritual good and evil.[1]

I don't know if you have ever thought much about the process of breathing. I guarantee you, there is not a time you remember not doing it—and you have done it tens of thousands of times every day of your life. It is in fact an involuntary action. Unless you have a pulmonary disease, you don't have to concentrate on breathing at all.

Have you ever considered why we breathe? One of the main functions of breathing is in the exchange of gases between the lungs and the blood. When breathing in, your lungs bring a much-needed oxygen supply to your bloodstream. Capillaries in the lungs take the oxygen and move it into blood cells where it is shipped out to various parts of the body and into the cells and tissue.

This transportation of oxygen throughout the body systems is the feeding process needed for your body to be living and healthy.

But, that's not all breathing does. As the cells release the oxygen into the tissue, it also collects the waste product—carbon dioxide—moving it back to the lungs and allowing it to escape the body.

Just as continual respiration is necessary for the physical body, this kind of continual respiration is a necessity for spiritual life. God acts on the soul; the soul re-acts to God.

The combined respiration is a process the body continually replays tens of thousands of times a day. There is a rhythm to breathing: taking oxygen in and letting carbon dioxide out. If either part stops, you die.

Just as your body has this life-giving rhythm, so your soul must have a life-giving rhythm of its own—a spiritual respiration, if you will. Breathe in God's grace, breathe out God's grace. In *The Great Privilege of those That are Born of God*, John Wesley described it like this:

> *Now one who is so born of God, as hath been above described, who continually receives into his soul the breath of life from God, the gracious influence of his Spirit, and continually renders it back; one who thus believes and loves, who by faith perceives the continual actings of God upon his spirit, and by a kind of spiritual re-action returns the grace he receives, in unceasing love, and praise, and prayer.*"[2]

Just as continual respiration is necessary for the physical body, this kind of continual respiration is a necessity for spiritual life. God acts on the soul; the soul re-acts to God. God breathes His life into the soul of man, and the soul returns the grace—surrenders the life—back to God in love, praise, and prayer.

In this way, the Christian experiences the presence of God. Notice that Wesley said,

> *who by faith perceives the continual actings of God upon his spirit...*

God is acting on the soul. It is His action first. We don't take the first step; He does. That is grace. But that action is perceived. We feel it. We know it happens. If God acts on your soul, why wouldn't you know it?

What would God's acting feel like? Peace? Love? Power? Yes, all these and more.

And what is the result? What do the actings of God on the soul do? Wesley said,

> *And by this new kind of spiritual respiration, spiritual life is not only sustained, but increased day by day...*

This is spiritual life. This is the way we relate to Him and He relates to us—spiritual respiration.

Wesley said spiritual respiration is how you "sustain" spiritual life. Probably one of the toughest things about a relationship with God is sustaining it.

Starting a relationship with God is not hard; He does that. You can't impress Him, entice Him, trick Him, or somehow make Him love you more.[3] But God in His grace moves toward you. He draws you, invites you to trust Him. He imparts His life to you and gives you His love. This is all God's work. All you do is receive it.

This is spiritual life. This is the way we relate to Him and He relates to us – spiritual respiration.

That's one of the problems with it; we try to make it something we do, and it is simply something He does.

> *But to all who did receive Him, He gave them the right to be children of God, to those who believe in His name, who were born, not of blood, or of the will of the flesh, or of the will of man, but of God.[4]*

There are two major issues with those who struggle with receiving grace: either you don't feel that you need it, or you don't feel that you deserve it.

Let me address those two issues. The first one is easy—you do need it. You without grace is... well, it is all you, and that is not enough.

We don't like to think that we need someone outside ourselves. We want to be self-sufficient. The sooner you recognize that you need God's grace, the sooner you get to where you're going. There is, however, a connection between self-centeredness, self-righteousness, and self-sufficiency. And while we might exalt self-sufficiency, we know self-centeredness and self-righteousness are not in God's will for us. Neither is self-sufficiency. The Bible calls it pride and idolatry.

On the second issue—the thought that you don't deserve it—well, the reality is, you don't. You never will; that's why it's grace. You have to surrender your unworthiness to His over-whelming graciousness and simply receive it. Remember that Jesus did what He did for us before we were saints. In fact, the Apostle Paul said we were the opposite:

> *But God proves His own love for us in that while we were still sinners, Christ died for us!*[5]

Receive grace as one who is unworthy yet needy.

Again, starting a relationship with God is easy because He has done everything for us.

> *For while we were still helpless, at the appointed moment, Christ died for the ungodly. For rarely will someone die for a just person—though for a good person perhaps someone might even dare to die. But God proves His own love for us in that while we were still sinners, Christ died for us! Much more then, since we have now been declared righteous by His blood, we will be saved through Him from wrath.*

> *For if, while we were enemies, we were reconciled to God through the death of His Son, then how much more, having been rec-onciled, will we be saved by His life! And not only that, but we also rejoice in God through our Lord Jesus Christ. We have now received this reconciliation through Him.*[6]

But—and here is the point of this chapter—once a person receives God's grace and responds to the drawings of God, rela-tionship becomes a two-way street. A relationship is always that, isn't it? It takes two to tango. A relationship is about shar-ing life, and that takes at least two.

And by this new kind of spiritual respiration, spiritual life is not only sustained, but increased day by day...

Sustaining a relationship is hard work. Someone said, "After every wedding comes a marriage." I think too many brides are in love with getting married. Then, after the magic and splendor of the perfect wedding is over, they have to deal with the person they married.

Relationships take daily care and maintenance. The same is true about your relationship with God.

Having a sustained intimate relationship with God is not impossible – it does take work though.

God's love for you does not wane, but your experience of it can. And certainly, your active love for Him can. How do you keep it hot? How do you keep it passionate and lively? It will take a daily interaction—a rhythm of receiving and releasing—a back and forth of God moving and you responding.

This is the key to intimacy with God: you receiving His love and responding back to Him.

When people become dull in their relationship with God—when they experience that cooling down of passion—they often look up and ask "Where is God?"

I am sure you have heard that old illustration about the elderly couple driving down the road. He sits behind the steering wheel and she sits up against the passenger side door. She looks over at him and says "You know, I don't know what happened to us. We used to sit right up against each other." The husband answers dryly, "I haven't moved."

If your relationship with God seems more distant than it was, ask yourself, "Who moved?"

Spiritual life is like the tide; I call it the ebb and flow of spiritual life. You can be on top of the mountain, experiencing the presence and power of God. Then, as suddenly as it came, that experience can be gone—not because God moved, or for some reason stopped loving you, but because you neglected something.

You let something go.

You stopped relating.

You forgot to breathe.

Having a sustained intimate relationship with God is not impossible. It does take work though.

Jesus used the example of a grape vine:

> *"I am the true vine, and My Father is the vineyard keeper... Remain in Me, and I in you. Just as a branch is unable to produce fruit by itself unless it remains on the vine, so neither can you unless you remain in Me... If anyone does not remain in Me, he is thrown aside like a branch and he withers.*[7]

Do you see what Jesus says here? The only way to have life and be productive is to remain in Him, to stay in constant and intimate relationship. Without that, there is only fruitlessness and withering—two words that perfectly describe a person who is wondering what happened to his spiritual life.

Have you ever thought about the difference between the two seas in Israel? They both are fed by the Jordan River. The Sea of Galilee is vibrant and teeming with life. The Dead Sea is not. What is the difference? The Sea of Galilee takes in water and releases water; the Dead Sea takes in water and does not release it. It is a dead end.

Have you ever tried to relate to someone who did not respond? You talk; they just sit there. You are trying your best to engage them; they just sit there. It is like hitting your head on a brick wall. Imagine what happens when God gives, but we don't respond or interact with Him. A sustained relationship is a two-way communication of life and love.

Not only does relationship with God sustain spiritual life, but victory in daily Christian living and spiritual growth are also dependent on it.

And by this new kind of spiritual respiration, spiritual life is not only sustained, but increased day by day...

Are you experiencing a daily increase in your spiritual life? Are you moving forward, going deeper, or reaching higher on a daily basis? Remember, the Christian life is not just about a one-time event of forgiveness; it involves transformation—and transformation takes relationship.

Too often Christians have tried to gain spiritual victory and growth by being disciplined, without having a personal, intimate relationship with God. They study hard. They practice spiritual disciplines. They sacrifice and suffer in order to become something.

If spiritual victory and growth could occur by your own effort, it wouldn't be spiritual, would it? The answer is in the Spirit—His work and presence in you. And that is a relationship.

One last thing: relationships should not stay the same. There should be continual growth and expansion of life and love. That is true in human relationships and it is certainly true about your relationship with God.

A love that is stagnant stinks! Friendships go stale. Marriages go cold. Spiritual life gets boring.

Your relationship with God should never get so comfortable that you stop growing in it.

The remedy? Don't get comfortable. Don't stop growing. A relationship is not an historical event. This is not about what happened 10 or 20 years ago. Relationships are about the present.

Growth and expansion of a relationship means there is a constant exploration, a deepening of sharing and an intimacy that allows you to continually grow in trust and faith.

This is especially true of your relationship with God. Your relationship with God should never get so comfortable that you stop growing in it. If you can only speak of your spiritual life in the past tense... you may not be breathing.

CHAPTER THREE

Breathe It In

What are the ingredients of a good relationship? Certainly, communication would be one of the chief elements. Communication allows for sharing, and sharing leads to intimacy.

The question for us is "How do I communicate with God?" Obviously, there are some barriers—He is eternal, we are temporal; He is spirit, we are physical. And yet, here is the key: we are also spiritual beings. God has created us in His image and part of that includes the ability to have a spiritual connection to Him.

Spiritual life (and thus relationship with God) consists of our breathing in God's grace and breathing out God's grace. Our ability to interact with Him this way is not based on our goodness or worthiness. We can attain this, not because we can reach that high, but because God has reached that low.

I have a friend who likes to say that "the first thing we find in the scripture is that God is a God who creates and communicates." How true! He not only walked and spoke with Adam, He breathed His life into Him! That was the beginning of what we find to be the biblical pattern for God—He constantly reaches down to us.

We see this pattern lived out in the relationship between God and Israel, and in the New Testament more fully in the coming of Jesus.

God has created us in His image and part of that includes the ability to have a spiritual connection to Him.

It is God's nature to share Himself. In reaching down to us, God offers us multiple ways by which we can be in a personal, intimate relationship with Him. These ways of relating are called "the Means of Grace."

The title "Means of Grace" tells us that these are not grace themselves, as if they are the end result. They are only a means to an end—the end being receiving and interacting with the grace of God.

John Wesley described the Means of Grace this way:

> By "means of grace" I understand outward signs, words, or actions, ordained of God, and appointed for this end, to be the ordinary channels whereby He might convey to men, preventing, justifying, or sanctifying grace... The chief of these means are prayer, whether in secret or with the great congregation; searching the Scriptures; (which implies reading, hearing, and meditating thereon;) and receiving the Lord's Supper, eating bread and drinking wine in remembrance of Him: And these we believe to be ordained of God, as the ordinary channels of conveying His grace to the souls of men.[1]

Ordinary channels of grace. There are certainly more ways than listed here, but these are the ordinary or common ways

God has given us (for consistent use) to experience Him: Prayer, Bible Study, and the Sacrament. We might broaden "sacrament" in our context by using the word Worship.[2]

While worship is certainly a broader term, the practices of sacrament, and even beyond that into fasting and shared Christian life, are found within the overarching system of corporate worship.

In order for a spiritual life to be sustained and growing, a person needs to practice the ordinary means of grace as a consistent part of their daily life. That's pretty simple; pray, read, and worship—breathe it in. Breathe in the life-giving, life-changing grace of God.[3] Not only does the presence of God's grace change you, but by practicing the means of grace you are reaching outside yourself to receive from God, and with that you are turned inside out. You will find that you are not sufficient, secure, or satisfied in and of yourself. And that is the beginning of a changed life.

The Means of Grace: Prayer

Wesley began his list of the means of grace with prayer. What exactly is prayer? Is it a time for you to tell God what He should do? Is it manipulation? Is it time for a grocery list of wants and needs? I am afraid too many Christians see it that way.

Allow me to give you the bigger picture. Prayer is a conversation. A two-way sharing of life between you and God. However, He is God and you are not. That's why I say, the majority of your time in prayer should be spent surrendering to God's will.

Don't get me wrong—God wants to hear your heart. He wants you to come to Him with your fears and desires. But His will is perfect. His timing is right. His heart and hands are working for your best. When you believe that, you can trust Him. And when you can trust Him, you can surrender to Him.[4]

How does prayer work as a means of grace? Maybe the answer is best seen in the simplest definition of the word: Prayer is talking with God.

Here is where we miss it. We often tell Christians they should pray every day, but if we see prayer just as a daily exercise it becomes mundane and a dead ritual.

"Now I lay me down to sleep. I pray the Lord my soul to keep."

If prayer is talking to the Eternal God—the Holy One — then how could prayer be anything less than exhilarating!

Here's the key—Prayer is not about controlling God. It is about learning to know the God Who is in control. Prayer is not ritual; it is relationship.

Prayer is not just an exercise we do to practice patience. Prayer is entering into a conversation that is already taking place. Paul tells us in Romans 8 that God draws us into His conversation through the Spirit's presence.

> *In the same way the Spirit also joins to help in our weakness, because we do not know what to pray or as we should, but the Spirit Himself intercedes for us with unspoken groanings. And He who searches the hearts knows the Spirit's mind-set, because He intercedes for the saints according to the will of God.[5]*

In other words, the Spirit of God, who knows the will of God, knows what should be prayed. Don't come to God with a list of things you want Him to do; let God reveal to you what He wants to do.

In this, prayer is not about you, but it is about the One to whom you are praying. He is already working, and He is working for your good. He wants to draw you into what He is doing, so He invites you into prayer.

Prayer falls into three distinct categories. First, there is worshipful prayer. Sometimes when you pray, you just pour out praise and honor to God. In fact, I suggest you start that way for a couple of reasons. It is a great way to pull your mind in from the things that would distract you. Also, it puts you in the mindset of prayer. But what better way to prioritize and understand your needs in any situation than to first put God in His place as your Creator, Father, Healer, etc.? Worshipful prayer re-orients your heart and mind.

The majority of your time in prayer should be spent surrendering to God's will.

In Psalm 77, the Psalmist is struggling. He is groaning and weak. He cannot even sleep. But then he turns his situation by remembering what God has done.

> *I will remember the Lord's works;*
> *yes, I will remember Your ancient wonders.*
> *I will reflect on all You have done*
> *and meditate on Your actions.*[6]

When you remember what God has done in the past, you have confidence in what He can and will do in the present and future. Worship changes everything. Worship will certainly change your prayer life.

A second distinct category in prayer is what I call sharing prayer. After a time of worship and praise, move to an honest time of sharing with God. Don't make the common mistake in thinking you can hide something from God.

God already knows your heart – but He also wants to hear it. By sharing your heart with Him you let down the walls and open up to His grace. Get personal. Get real. Pour out your cares and concerns. Let God hear your pain. Then and only then will you be able to hear His healing voice.

Finally, there is a third category—surrendered prayer. We see this best illustrated in the prayer of Jesus in the Garden of Gethsemane. He pours out His heart to the Father. He tells Him what He wants. He begs Him for relief. But then, in that moment of personal pain, Jesus surrenders His will to the will of the Father.

> *Then He withdrew from them about a stone's throw, knelt down, and began to pray, "Father, if You are willing, take this cup away from Me—nevertheless, not My will, but Yours, be done."*[7]

Start prayer by putting God in His place through worship. Then, give Him your heart. Share with Him what you need or want. But come back to where you started, with God in His place as King.[8] With your needs in hand, take them to His throne. Place them in His trustworthy hands, and rest in knowing Who He is.

---

*Prayer is not about controlling God,
it is about learning to know the God
Who is in control.*

Prayer in this way will change your life. I know, you pray for things to change, but you will be the thing most changed by your prayer life.

Reaching outward and upward to God's power and grace in prayer is the right posture, with the most potential to transform your life.

The Means of Grace: Scripture

Scripture is life-changing, not just because the words are wise and can train your heart and mind in the ways of God (which is important, by the way), but approaching scripture as the living word is a vital part of a relationship with the living God.

Wesley's term for how to use the scripture is "searching the scriptures." What does he mean by that? He defines it as "hearing, reading, and meditating" on the word.[9]

Hearing the scripture implies corporate scripture use: Preaching, Bible teaching, etc. A continual diet of audible scripture will shape your life, both internally and externally. The Spirit speaks through the word of God. Hear Him.

The second use is in reading the scripture. Reading the scripture, we understand. Again, the Spirit speaks through the word of God. The most interesting part of scripture is its ability to speak over and over again into a person's life. Those who have read it most never tire of it because of this "living" aspect. The scripture can speak to your life if you will listen.

Thirdly, Wesley says that we should meditate on the scripture. What does this imply? The scripture is not to be a casual part of our life; it is to be the very heartbeat of who we are. We should be people of the word. The scripture is meant to be both understood and applied. A casual reading will not do.

As with prayer, when approaching scripture you are entering into a conversation that has already been going on. For centuries, the stories and message of the Bible have transformed lives and shaped the hearts and minds of God's people. You enter into that history when you open the book.

Not only that, but the same Spirit that inspired the scripture meets you in the reading, studying, and meditating on it. Interacting with the inspired word is, in effect, interacting with the Spirit. That is life-changing.

Imagine the impact of scripture when for the first time a person prayerfully looks to God to speak and teach—and for the first time he shifts his allegiance from his own wisdom and power to that of God. Scripture has become in that moment a means of grace. He has been turned inside out. Now, imagine doing that every day for 30, 40, or 50 years.

...the same Spirit that inspired the scripture meets you in the reading, studying and meditating on it. Interacting with the inspired Word is in effect, interacting with the Spirit.

Reaching out and up through scripture will change your life.

Every person must find his or her own way of relating to God through scripture. I suggest you include a couple of basic principles:

First, approach the word as a love letter. I know, some of it is heavy and difficult, but God has given it to us to communicate something. That desire for communication itself is love. Spend time with the One who loves you enough to speak to you from His life.

Second, study the word. Don't make the mistake of applying it before you know what it means. There are lots of helps both in the bookstore and online, but you would be best served by learning to study it yourself.

Do this: read it. Find the context of the specific passage. Research the individual Greek and Hebrew words used. Take the time to understand what God is saying in the text. All this can be assisted by commentaries and online sources, but don't get lazy. Study to show yourself approved![10] Learn some Inductive Bible Study skills.

Third, apply your study to your life. Meditate on it. Chew on it. Let it marinate in your soul. What does this text mean for you? Are you living it out? Why or why not? What needs to change in light of the text?

When you look into the word you find that it acts as a mirror for your soul. God will reveal Himself there, but He will also reveal you. Your attitudes and actions, as well as the impetus for them, will all be there. In that moment, God will speak some of the most intimate and life-changing words to you. But you have to be open to hearing Him.

The ancient practice of *Lectio Divina* is about praying and meditating on scripture. It has a similar rhythm to that of the breathing in and out. It involves taking in the text and then, in prayer, offering it back to God. We hear from Him, and we offer our confession. We ask Him for application, and we commit to the change. However you do it, don't let the point of the text pass you by. God is speaking. Are you listening?

Fourth, be sure to do scripture study and application with others. You weren't meant do this alone. The story of the scripture is a story of community. In community "iron sharpens iron."[11] In community we share life, and with it the burden of encouragement and strengthening each other.

The word is most powerful when you study it yourself and you are having it applied by others at the same time. Listen to your pastor. Listen to your teachers. The scripture is plain about that. Listen to your Christian friends who can also shed light on God's word to you.

Above all, listen to God. 98% of what He will ever say to you is found in the scriptures. Seek His voice there. Hear His heart there. Allow Him to breathe into you there.

The Means of Grace: Worship

By the general term "worship" I mean the multi-faceted actions of worship, sometimes called liturgy. The word "liturgy" literally means "work of the people." These actions are a part of the physical working out of your relationship with God. Fasting, sacrament, and other corporate aspects of Church life are all a part of worship as a means of grace.

In an age when the Church is not seen as so important— even to those who claim to love God— the question is asked, "How does going to Church act as a means of grace?"

Breathing in God's grace through regular, committed Church fellowship is absolutely one of the most powerful ways God shapes your spiritual life.

In the Church, you can find the grace of God at work. What you do with it will determine the impact it has on your life.

Church is meant to be more than a drive-by hearing of a sermon. It is more than singing worship songs and giving in the offering. Christ gave us the Church to gather us into the life-giving fellowship of His body. Nourishment is found there. Encouragement is gained there. Mission and ministry is learned there.

In the Church, you can find the grace of God at work. What you do with it will determine the impact it has on your life. The sermon, singing, scripture, praying, and giving of a Sunday morning Church service can change your life if you participate with them in the breathing in of God's grace.

In the liturgy of the Church, we celebrate the Lord's Supper. The Lord's Supper is about stopping in our tracks, focusing on His gift of life to us, and recognizing our unworthiness of it. The sacrament reorients our hearts and minds to understand who we are and Who God is—a people in need of God's grace and a God who gives Himself to us in grace.

It is in the Lord's Supper that we as a community share a common need and a common Savior. Use that time to examine your life. Paul said,

So a man should examine himself; in this way he should eat the bread and drink from the cup.[12]

Growing up as a Roman Catholic, I learned a liturgical response to the self-examination of Communion. We all said together, "I am not worthy to receive you, but only say the word and I shall be healed." I still come to communion saying that.

Breathe in God's grace in the Lord's Supper.

The liturgy also includes various forms of fasting or abstinence. This sometimes has been a controversial means of grace. Over the years, some Christians have practiced extreme fasting, and others have made it into some sort of yearly diet plan. It has at times been unproductive to the biblical call to fast.

Fasting, or some form of abstinence, is a way for us to practice saying "No" to our desires. And as the monks said in the past, "when we discipline our body we discipline our soul." You may need to find a way to fast other than in eating, such as fasting from some of our current electronic fascinations or from some other area of your life that distracts you.

But fasting is more than practice. Fasting is a way for God to speak. In the silence of our suffering we can open our ears to God's voice. Without the things that distract us from God, our ears are more attuned to Him.

I remember spending some time alone in England during my studies there. I had a little room above the library at a small college, just big enough for a bed and desk. And if I were there during the summer months, there were times when I was absolutely alone. Being a people person, that was hard. But I heard from God during that time. I even determined that it would probably be good for ministers to find a few weeks alone every year. (I haven't practiced that yet.)

While observing your fast you might find obeying God to be easier. After all, if you can't say "No" to your own desires, will you be able to say "Yes" to God's when it's hard to? Fasting teaches us to hear and obey.

Lastly, let me say something about other Christians as a means of grace. An important part of this understanding of worship is that we do it corporately. Other Christians in the body of Christ are one of the ways God speaks, teaches, and shapes you.

This is one of the ways the drive-by Church attender misses out on the grace of God offered them in the Church. That's why Paul, when writing to the Church at Ephesus about the One Body, said we should do this:

> *Speaking to one another in psalms, hymns, and spiritual songs, singing and making music from your heart to the Lord, giving thanks always for everything to God the Father in the name of our Lord Jesus Christ, submitting to one another in the fear of Christ.*[13]

"One another"—that phrase is used 100 times in the New Testament. Sixty-Nine of those times it is used to show us how we are to treat each other. One third of the uses tell us to love each other.

God wants us to think of ourselves as a part of something bigger than ourselves. We belong to each other.

There is definitely a point to be seen. God wants us to think of ourselves as a part of something bigger than ourselves. We belong to each other.

Hebrews chapter 10 demonstrates the need for our being an active part of the Body of Christ. When the Book of Hebrews was written, there were a group of Christians in Rome who, under a second persecution, had begun to step away from their confession of faith.

The author of this letter knew that the answer to their fear was not to be found in the individual Christian attempting to be strong apart from the Church. Instead he encouraged them to hold to their faith as a part of the Church, corporately, where they could help others and be helped by others.

> *Let us hold on to the confession of our hope without wavering, for He who promised is faithful. And let us be concerned about one another in order to promote love and good works, not staying away from our worship meetings, as some habitually do, but encouraging each other, and all the more as you see the day drawing near.*[14]

You weren't meant to take this journey alone. The Church is God's way of bringing us into fellowship with others who are sharing in His grace.

The Church is a place to both breathe in God's grace, and breathe out God's grace, as we will see in the next chapter.

CHAPTER FOUR

Breathe It Out

Breathing is a two-way action. If you cease to either breathe in or breathe out, you will die. Both are equally important.

When John Wesley described spiritual respiration, he spoke of both actions. The Christian must "receive into his soul the breath of life from God, the gracious influence of his Spirit, and continually render it back."

Both the receiving and the rendering are important, and both must be consistent. But, how do you "render back to God" the breath he gives you?

> *...it is continually rendered back by love, by prayer, and praise, and thanksgiving; love and praise, and prayer being the breath of every soul which is truly born of God.*[1]

Breathing in the grace of God refocuses your heart away from yourself and turns it outward. Rather than depending on your own self-sufficient power, you now look to God for wisdom, grace, forgiveness, help, etc.

Breathing out the grace of God continues that process. Thankfulness of heart, and praise and love toward God changes the attitude. Wesley's three categories of breathing out—love, praise, and prayer—constitute for him the very "breath of every soul which is truly born of God." That is how we breathe out. We draw in His breath (that is, the grace of God), and we release back our breath through love, praise, and prayer.

Wesley rightly described our breathing out as a reaction of our soul when acted on by God.

> *...who by faith perceives the continual actings of God upon his spirit, and by a kind of spiritual re-action returns the grace he receives, in unceasing love, and praise, and prayer.*[2]

There is no boasting of our love for Him; it is a reaction of our soul to the grace of God poured out in it. The same is true of our praise and prayer. All these come from the work of God in us and are not to be attributed to us as our own works.

This is a spiritual reaction. Take a moment to consider the word "react." Breathing out is not about attempting to act toward God; it is merely allowing the soul to respond to the grace of God.

Isn't it amazing that God made us in His image? He created us to react to Him. Just as the life of the Father is given to the Son, and the Son reciprocates by offering His life and love back to the Father—that picture of Trinitarian shared life is how and what we are made to be.

The reaction of our soul in breathing out is as natural to our existence as our lungs breathing out carbon dioxide. And by the way, while breathing in oxygen is a great thing, not breathing out the by-product, carbon dioxide, is poison to your system.

Notice that when Wesley described the process he used the word "continually" twice:

The Spirit or breath of God is immediately inspired, breathed into the new-born soul; and the same breath which comes from, returns to, God: As it is continually received by faith, so it is continually rendered back by love, by prayer, and praise, and thanksgiving..

It takes both God's acting and our reacting to complete the process of spiritual respiration, and both must be a continual part of who we are. A life consistent in these things experiences not only the grace of God, but growth in that grace.

Going back to the picture of the Trinitarian life, we are created to reflect the shared life of God. The same life shared in the Son is shared in us.

There is no boasting of our love for Him—it is a reaction of our soul to the grace of God poured out in it. The same is true of our praise and prayer. All these come from the work of God in us and are not to be attributed to us as our own works.

This is the foundation of relationship with God. But it takes an expanded understanding of grace to see this. Grace is not merely God's attitude toward us (unmerited favor), it is also the action of God toward us (shared life).

Grace is not just your sins being overlooked; grace is your being invaded by the presence of God.

Breathing out, then, is our response to God's actions. God reaches toward us with grace; we react with love, praise, and prayer.

Breathing Out: Love

The first aspect of breathing out given us by Wesley is love. The scripture tells us that love is a reaction. The Apostle John said,

We love because He first loved us.[3]

Could it be that those who don't love God, just haven't experienced or recognized His love for them yet? Love for God comes from a heart that is loved by God. It is the natural reaction to His action toward us.

I once had a student who never felt loved by her often-absent Father. He was always working, never giving her the quality time she needed from him. When studying about the various ways we show and receive love, she realized her father was expressing love for her the only way he knew how—through his sacrificial work schedule. Parenting skills aside, his love—while real for his daughter—was not experienced by her, because it was not recognized as love.

I wonder how often God's love has gone unrecognized as such.[4] Breathing out is both a reaction to and an expression of our recognizing His love for us. Love happens in two distinct but related directions; some people liken it to a cross made up of both vertical and horizontal beams. First, grace brings a reaction of the soul toward God. Here is the process: If you are breathing in—that is, your prayers are worshipping, sharing, and surrendering; you are hearing, studying, and meditating on scripture; and you are engaged in worship with a group of Christians who are encouraging and shaping you—you are on the receiving end of relating to the living God. He is giving, sharing, and pouring His life into you. You will hear from Him. You will learn from Him. Through the fellowship of others, you will experience His love and care.

You will "feel" something. You will experience spiritual life, spiritual growth, and God's presence in your life. Love at its base level, then, is the emotional reaction of the soul because God is meeting your needs, sharing Himself with you, and is relate-ably present.

Christ doesn't command us to love one another because it is the easy thing to do. Christ commands us to love one another because He has poured out His love in our hearts through the Holy Spirit.

A second level of love toward God, a much deeper one, occurs as you become increasingly aware of what He has done on your behalf in the work of Christ. That love-reaction is the relational basis for saving faith. Love on this level will be about devotion. It will lead you to sacrifice all, to give all to the One who gave Himself for you.

This is breathing out. Love toward God has become the very breath of the Christian. It is natural—as natural as breathing out carbon dioxide thousands of times a day.

While a vertical love toward God is foundational to Christian living, the New Testament is clear that it doesn't stop there.

There is a horizontal love—a love toward others that is also a reaction to grace.

With God's love and grace applied to your heart by the Holy Spirit, love toward others becomes more natural for you. This is not a love based on their meeting your needs or even for some other humanitarian reason. Breathing out love toward others is about allowing the love of God to be reflected in your reaction toward them. It is literally allowing God to love them through you.

Jesus said,

> *I give you a new command: Love one another. Just as I have loved you, you must also love one another. By this all people will know that you are My disciples, if you have love for one another.*[5]

You have probably heard the old adage, "The proof of the pudding is in the eating."

Because of His example of loving others, and because of our experience of having His love in us, our love for others proves our relationship with Jesus.

Love others because Jesus said to.

Love others because you want to imitate Him.

Love others to prove you belong to Him.

But above all else, love others because you are loved by Him.

You can't give away what you don't have any more than you can come back from where you haven't been. Christ doesn't command us to love one another because it is the easy thing to do. Christ commands us to love one another because He has already poured out His love in our hearts through the Holy Spirit.[6]

Loving God and loving others is simply breathing out what God has already breathed into you. You simply have to let that which God puts in you, be a movement of grace from God, through you, to others. There is no greater expression of our love for God than in sharing His love for others.

When John Wesley was describing the works necessary for Sanctification, he gave two types. First, you must be consistent in the means of grace. That is, you must be breathing in God's grace. But secondly, in order to experience the sanctifying grace of God, you must be consistent in ministering to others. This is breathing out. Whether it is spiritual or physical, Christians should reach out with God's love and grace. [7]

Wesley felt so strongly about those two types of works that he warned without them, you could not even stay where you are spiritually, let alone move forward or grow. They are necessary.

> *It is incumbent on all that are justified to be zealous of good works. And these are so necessary, that if a man willingly neglect them, he cannot reasonably expect that he shall ever be sanctified; he cannot grow in grace, in the image of God, the mind which was in Christ Jesus; nay, he cannot retain the grace he has received; he cannot continue in faith, or in the favour of God. What is the inference we must draw herefrom, Why, that both repentance, rightly understood, and the practice of all good works, --works of piety, as well as works of mercy (now properly so called, since they spring from faith), are, in some sense, necessary to sanctification.[8]*

Serving others from a heart that is loved is not only the basis of Christian living; it is a necessity for a Christian's life.

Breathing Out: Praise

Just as love is the very breath of a Christian, praise, too, is an expression of our response to grace.

When speaking of the movement of life from the Father to the Son, St. Augustine described the life of God—that is the Spirit of God—as the ecstasy of love between the two. He is more than love, but the Spirit is the overflowing part of God that pours out from Him, in love for others.

Praise acts that way for us. It is the ecstasy, the overflowing reaction of the soul toward God. He works in us—we praise. Praise is the very breath of the Christian, expelling thankfulness from a heart touched by grace.

Loving God and loving others is simply breathing out what God has already breathed into you.

The scripture speaks of praise through words, singing, and music. Many times, musical instruments are mentioned. Sometimes praise occurs in the silence of the moment. However it is accomplished, praise is a reaction of the soul to God.

Praise is based on thankfulness and is due God based on what He has done and Who He is.

Praise is also good for you.

In the process of breathing, expelling carbon dioxide is absolutely necessary. Carbon dioxide is a byproduct of oxygen being pumped into the body's system; but as I said earlier, it is poisonous to you. It has got to go. Breathing out is essential for life.

> *Praise is the ecstasy, the overflowing reaction of the soul toward God.*

Praise, too, is good for you. Praise changes things. When life clouds your view, or the storms of life roll in and darken everything around you, praise will change your perspective. When you can see no good thing around you, and there is no end in sight, praise will shed a light in the darkness.

Praise is how you jump-start a life turn-around. It changes your mindset; it sets your perspective and priorities around what God has done and not what life has dealt you.

> *Our adoration of God is encapsulated in a prayerful return of His love for us.*

Praise will shift your eyes away from the problem to the solution. It is like the reaction of your mind when you start to feel the first drops of rain in a storm. As soon as the drops begin to fall, you look for shelter. Praise is that shift—the thankfulness you express even in the storms of life. As soon as you praise, you will begin to experience the presence of God that was already there—your shelter in the storm.

Praise expels the poison. The negative attitudes, critical speaking, and over-whelming sense of doom fade as praise begins.

Breathing Out: Prayer

In the previous chapter, we discussed prayer as a means

of breathing in God's grace. If you are praying in a process of worshipping (putting God in His place), sharing (pouring out your heart to God), and surrendering (acceptance of God's will), you will find that a fourth type of prayer also naturally occurs: adoration.

The God you worship is all-powerful. The God you share your heart with in prayer is a loving Father. The God to whom you surrender also gives Himself to you. He interacts with you and shares His life with you. Like any good Father, He loves to hear His children say, "I love you."

Remember, the very purpose of our creation was to reflect the reciprocation of love between the Father and the Son. Returned love is the essence of why we exist. In breathing out in prayer we live out the very reason for our existence.

Prayer may be one of the most significant acts of humanity. Our adoration of God is encapsulated in a prayerful return of His love for us.

With adoration comes another type of prayer: Supplication. In breathing out in prayer, we think of others. Adoration focuses us on our vertical relationship with God, but the horizontal relationship between us and others is also a powerful guide in prayer.

The Apostle Paul said,

> *Do nothing out of rivalry or conceit, but in humility consider others as more important than yourselves. Everyone should look out not only for his own interests, but also for the interests of others.*[9]

Praying for others will move your interest from "self" to "serve." True supplication doesn't just see a need and ask God to meet it. As James 2:14-17 tells us, that kind of faith—maybe even that kind of prayer—is dead. We reach out, both in prayer and in service, because our hearts are turned outward. That is the true power of breathing out.

CHAPTER FIVE

Just Breathe

Relationships can have an ebb and flow to them. There are times when the passion, intimacy, and commitment are hot, and there are times when they are less so. The difference is usually found in the neglecting of some key element of relationship.

The same is true about your relationship with God. There are mountains and there are valleys. There will be those mountain-top moments when God seems so real you could reach out and touch Him and your love for Him cannot be swayed. And then there are the valleys. You will wonder where He went. You will seek and not find. Your distractedness will bring a weakness to your love for Him. And there, in that low place, you will struggle to do the things you had determined in your heart to do.

But spiritual weakness and shipwrecks of faith do not happen in a moment of strength. John Wesley's sermon *The Great Privilege of Those that are Born of God* details the steps taken in falling away from God. It is not natural for a Christian to walk away from Him who gives us life. But we know it does happen; unfortunately, it is not impossible for a Christian to drift from a relationship with God.

In Revelation chapter 2, Jesus rebuked the Church at Ephesus, not for evil practices or bad theology.

> *I know your works, your labor, and your endurance, and that you cannot tolerate evil. You have tested those who call themselves apostles and are not, and you have found them to be liars. You also possess endurance and have tolerated many things because of My name and have not grown weary.[1]*

In fact, their practices were praiseworthy. It was their relationship with God that was not right.

> *But I have this against you: You have abandoned the love you had at first.[2]*

It's easier to do something *for* God than to relate *with* God. We can fight for what is right and still not be right with Him. It was Thomas Aquinas who prayed,

> *Lord, in my zeal for the love of truth, let me not forget the truth about love.[3]*

The Church at Ephesus had focused on orthodoxy, and not their relationship with Jesus. The believers there had done all the right things and neglected the one thing God wants most from each of us—an intimate relationship of shared life and love.

It is not natural for a Christian to walk away from Him who gives us life.

It is possible to miss it; we all are susceptible to the distractions and defilements of this world.

Watch out, brothers, so that there won't be in any of you an evil, unbelieving heart that departs from the living God. But encourage each other daily, while it is still called today, so that none of you is hardened by sin's deception.[4]

Sin's Deception

It would be unethical to tell you that once you are a Christian your life gets easier, that spiritual life comes naturally, or that spiritual warfare has now ended. On the contrary, when you entered into a relationship with God, your spiritual battles began to deepen. And in the midst of the battle, sin's deception is always at work, attempting to draw you away from God.

You must be diligent. You must be disciplined. And that is what this chapter is about.

In *The Great Privilege of Those who are Born of God*, John Wesley addressed a difficult passage of scripture about Christians and sin.

The Apostle John tells us,

Everyone who has been born of God does not sin, because His seed remains in him; he is not able to sin because he has been born of God.[5]

Those are strong words.

He does not sin.

He is not able to sin.

The problem is, we know that a Christian is still susceptible to the deceit of sin; the Book of Hebrews was written to a group of Christians struggling with this. Under a second persecution, they had begun to step back from their relationship to

Christ. The author warns his audience multiple times to hold their confidence to the end, to beware of the hardening of the heart against grace.

> *Watch out, brothers, so that there won't be in any of you an evil, unbelieving heart that departs from the living God. But encourage each other daily, while it is still called today, so that none of you is hardened by sin's deception. For we have become companions of the Messiah if we hold firmly until the end the reality that we had at the start.[6]*

And yet John says,

> *Everyone who has been born of God does not sin*

and

> *he is not able to sin.*

What is the answer to this seemingly contradictory textual problem? Wesley explains,

> *I answer, what has been long observed is this: so long as "he that is born of God keepeth himself," (which he is able to do, by the grace of God,) "the wicked one toucheth him not:" But if he keepeth not himself, if he abide not in the faith, he may commit sin even as another man.[7]*

Here is the key—"as long as he keepeth himself." Neglect is the great enemy of your soul.

Neglect is deadly. Neglect leads to a sinking in the sea, even after Jesus bids you to walk on water.[8] Neglect is the branch being separated from the vine and not only bearing no fruit, but withering and being worthy of nothing but being burned up.[9]

John Wesley used King David as a perfect example of the process which takes place in a soul weakened by neglect. He was anointed by God, experienced the Holy Spirit, and yet fell into sin.

David's fall happened in stages, moved by missteps and wrong decisions.

> *He did not "keep himself," by that grace of God which was suffi-cient for him. He fell, step by step, First, into negative, inward sin, not "stirring up the gift of God which was in him," not "watching unto prayer," not "pressing on to the mark of the prize of his high calling:" Then, into positive inward sin, inclining to wickedness with his heart, giving way to some evil desire or temper: Next, he lost his faith, his sight of a pardoning God, and consequently his love of God; and, being then weak and like another man, he was capable of committing even outward sin.[10]*

Neglect is the great enemy of your soul.

When it comes to relating to God, you will find that neglect-ing the means of grace is the first step toward a cooling off of your passion, intimacy, and commitment toward Him.

You still believe. You still go through the motions of serving God and serving others. But what you end up with is more of the "doing" of religion and less of the "knowing" of relationship.

And religion is always easier than relationship. It can act as a façade. You look right, act right, and sound right. But religion can be deceiving. You can look right without your relationship with God being right.

Notice Wesley's process – first, you leave off the normal means of grace. You neglect prayer, studying the Bible, going to church. This is a deeper problem than just not doing these things; this is an inner sin of being spiritually lazy. And a lazy spiritual life leads to not only greater temptation, but greater weakness in temptation.

After the inner sin of laziness come the outward acts of sin. There is a basic process we see in life—laziness leads to sloppiness. Sloppiness leads to disaster. And for the Christian, it is a spiritual disaster.

What that means for Christians who are lazy with their spiritual lives is that they will eventually do things they swore they would never do.

That's how a Christian falls into sin. That's how he decides to forfeit grace. That's how he walks away from God's path and plan for him.

But our goal is not to go backwards or even stay where we are. We want to grow into all God has for us. We want the transformation of grace in our soul. We want to be remade in the image of God.

Spiritual Respiration must become a consistent, daily part of your life. You must make it a priority. Listen to the strong words of warning and encouragement used by the author of Hebrews:

> *We must, therefore, pay even more attention to what we have heard, so that we will not drift away.[11]*

> *Watch out, brothers, so that there won't be in any of you an evil, unbelieving heart that departs from the living God.[12]*

Therefore, while the promise to enter His rest remains, let us fear that none of you should miss it.[13]

Let us then make every effort to enter that rest, so that no one will fall into the same pattern of disobedience.[14]

Here are the words he used:

Pay attention.

Watch out.

Let us fear.

Let us make every effort.

And finally,

Demonstrate diligence so you won't become lazy.

Now we want each of you to demonstrate the same diligence for the final realization of your hope, so that you won't become lazy but will be imitators of those who inherit the promises through faith and perseverance.[15]

The author of Hebrews, under the inspiration of the Holy Spirit, felt there was something we need to do, a part we are to play in our daily relationship with God.

A diligent and intentional spiritual life—a daily breathing in and breathing out of God's grace—is imperative for a victorious Christian.

John Wesley wrote a letter concerning this to one of his preachers, John Trembath. Trembath had become spiritually derailed over his laziness and lack of discipline. Wesley said,

Certainly some years ago you was alive to God. You experienced the life and power of religion. And does not God intend that the trials you meet with should bring you back to this? You cannot stand still; you know this is impossible. You must go forward or backward. Either you must recover that power and be a Christian altogether, or in a while you will have neither power nor form, inside nor outside.[16]

John Trembath did not become derailed overnight. This was a gradual shift away from spiritual life. What were the steps to Trembath's spiritual condition? What happened? Wesley diagnosed Trembath's issue as being tied to his lack of reading, meditation, and prayer. Without these disciplines, there is a lack of depth both in your life and in your ministry practice, and in the end your spiritual life suffers.

What has exceedingly hurt you in time past, nay, and I fear to this day, is want of reading. I scarce ever knew a preacher read so little. And perhaps by neglecting it you have lost the taste for it. Hence your talent in preaching does not increase. It is just the same as it was seven years ago. It is lively, but not deep; there is little variety; there is no compass of thought. Reading only can supply this, with meditation and daily prayer. You wrong yourself greatly by omitting this. You can never be a deep preacher without it any more than a thorough Christian.[17]

If you find yourself to be in a spiritual malaise, you can recover your spiritual life. If you have never had the life and power that Wesley speaks of, you can gain it. Wesley's advice to Trembath is good for all of us.

O begin! Fix some part of every day for private exercises. Whether you like it or no, read and pray daily. It is for your life; there is no other way: else you will be a trifler all your days, and a pretty, superficial preacher. Do justice to your own soul; give it time and means to grow. Do not starve yourself any longer. Take up your cross, and be a Christian altogether. Then will all the children of God rejoice (not grieve) over you.[18]

Notice two very important words in this quote – "begin" and "daily." Without "daily exercise" you will only be a "trifler" with God and "a pretty superficial preacher." Daily interaction with God "is for your life." Otherwise, you are playing with God, not drawing life from God. And, Wesley said "begin." At some point you have to start. You have to set your focus on doing "justice to your own soul." Give it the "time and means to grow."

Daily Breathing and Sanctification

The intentional Christian life includes daily relating to God, corporate worship of God, as well as serving God through serving others.

Spiritual Respiration must become a consistent, daily part of your life. You must make it a priority.

This consistent process of reaching outside yourself is pre-scribed by John Wesley, first in the seeking and waiting for salvation. He described it this way:

All who desire the grace of God are to wait for it in the means He hath ordained...

And thus he continues in God's way, in hearing, reading, meditating, praying, and partaking of the Lord's Supper, till God, in the manner that pleases Him, speaks to his heart, "Thy faith hath saved thee. Go in peace."

> *Thus may we lead him, step by step, through all the means which God has ordained; not according to our own will, but just as the Providence and the Spirit of God go before and open the way.*[19]

Next, Wesley felt that spiritual life could not be maintained, let alone grow, without a consistent process of living in the means of grace and involvement in ministry.

> *It is generally supposed, that the means of grace and the ordinances of God are equivalent terms. We commonly mean by that expression, those that are usually termed, works of piety; viz., hearing and reading the Scripture, receiving the Lord's Supper, public and private prayer, and fasting.*

> *And it is certain these are the ordinary channels which convey the grace of God to the souls of men. But are they the only means of grace? Surely there are works of mercy, as well as works of piety, which are real means of grace. They are more especially such to those that perform them with a single eye. And those that neglect them, do not receive the grace which otherwise they might. Yea, and they lose, by a continued neglect, the grace which they had received. Is it not hence that many who were once strong in faith are now weak and feeble-minded?*

> *The walking herein is essentially necessary, as to the continuance of that faith whereby we are already saved by grace, so to the attainment of everlasting salvation.*[20]

Lastly, Wesley felt that while sanctification was a work of grace applied by faith, works of piety and works of mercy—in other words, the means of grace and ministry—were necessary to sanctification in the same way repentance was necessary to initial salvation.[21]

> *It is incumbent on all that are justified to be zealous of good works. And these are so necessary, that if a man willingly neglect them,*

he cannot reasonably expect that he shall ever be sanctified; he cannot grow in grace, in the image of God, the mind which was in Christ Jesus; nay, he cannot retain the grace he has received; he cannot continue in faith, or in the favour of God.

What is the inference we must draw herefrom, Why, that both repentance, rightly understood, and the practice of all good works, --works of piety, as well as works of mercy (now properly so called, since they spring from faith), are, in some sense, necessary to sanctification.

"But what good works are those, the practice of which you affirm to be necessary to sanctification?"

First, all works of piety; such as public prayer, family prayer, and praying in our closet; receiving the supper of the Lord; searching the Scriptures, by hearing, reading, meditating; and using such a measure of fasting or abstinence as our bodily health allows.

Secondly, all works of mercy; whether they relate to the bodies or souls of men; such as feeding the hungry, clothing the naked, entertaining the stranger, visiting those that are in prison, or sick, or variously afflicted; such as the endeavouring to instruct the ignorant, to awaken the stupid sinner, to quicken the lukewarm, to confirm the wavering, to comfort the feeble-minded, to succour the tempted, or contribute in any manner to the saving of souls from death.

This is the repentance, and these the "fruits meet for repentance," which are necessary to full sanctification. This is the way wherein God hath appointed His children to wait for complete salvation.[22]

For Wesley, there are two issues at work here. First, the means of grace are about interacting with the grace of God. When a person reads and studies the scripture, the same Spirit of God who inspired the writers meets with the reader. In prayer, we are speaking to and hearing from God. This interaction enlivens us. It draws us to God and away from sin.

But secondly, as believers our issues lie deeper than outward sin. We have a self-interested nature, a delusion of self-sovereignty, which has to be dealt with. This is about who we are in the core of our being.

Sin has bent our nature inward, and now we don't look much like our Creator. Left alone, our nature would not be self-giving like God's. And yet we were created to reflect His nature. The "curving in" of our nature (as St. Augustine described it) must be remedied if we are to fully reflect the life and love of God.

That's why salvation is not just about forgiveness but also renewal and restoration. Sanctification is about the grace of God transforming us "spirit, soul, and body."[23] But sanctification does not happen in a vacuum.

If the problem with us is inwardness and selfishness, how does God draw us into otherness and selflessness? That's where the whole process of breathing in and breathing out becomes powerful in the life of a believer.

Breathing in God's grace is about shifting your eyes away from yourself and focusing on God as the giver and you as the receiver. You learn to depend on Him and trust Him. Breathing out focuses on responding to God; through it you recognize God's place as giver of life. Then ministering to the needs of others both spiritually and physically, you are stretching outside yourself to care for someone besides yourself. You will begin to see them through the eyes of Jesus.

In this process, the end result is to be the outward drawing of your soul. God will confront you there.[24] He will arrest you with questions of your intention. "Why do you reach out? Is it for you or for others?" "Are you still clinging to your life or have you surrendered it?" The working out of the means of grace and ministry will reveal your wrong motives and attitudes, along with hidden pride.[25]

This is the disciple's path. This is where the soul opens up like a flower and experiences the grace of God in the deep places often untouched by the cross. As Wesley said,

> *This is the repentance, and these the "fruits meet for repentance," which are necessary to full sanctification. This is the way wherein God hath appointed His children to wait for complete salvation.*[26]

This is the path of the cross—to daily focus your heart outside yourself, to consistently and intentionally surrender yourself to the outward momentum of God's grace. To do this you will have to die to your own self-interest. This is the conflict of the soul which will cost you everything.

And that's why it must be a consistent, daily journey with God.

How do you make practices like Bible study and prayer, daily and consistent? First, you set aside the time. If you don't designate a particular portion of each day for the development of your spiritual life, you will be less likely to ever establish these essential elements of relationship with God.

Time is hard to come by. I once read a letter a lady wrote to a magazine editor asking for advice about finding time to pray. She said, "I can't find time to pray so I just do it while I do my morning run. Is that ok?" The editor wisely wrote back, "You can find time to run, but not to pray?" Our priorities are telling. Make prayer and Bible study a priority.

Second, once you have your time, set aside a place. I know, you can do these things anywhere. But will you? The best practice is to set aside a place where you are going to go to find time with God. Make it your place.

Third, set aside the tools. For instance, starting a physical fitness plan requires preparation. If you wait until your early morning wake-up call to locate the right clothes and equipment, you probably won't make your workout. The same is true for spiritual exercise. Gather your Bible, concordance, notebook, laptop or iPad, pens and other devotional books, in advance. That way, all you have to do is get to the place, and you are ready to begin.

Breathing in God's grace is about shifting your eyes away from yourself and focusing on God as the giver and you as the receiver. You learn to depend on Him and trust Him. Breathing out focuses on responding to God; through it you recognize God's place as giver of life.

Fourth, just do it—but not alone. Along with Bible study and prayer, you must make corporate worship a priority. If you don't actively and consistently participate in a local church, you must settle that issue immediately. Going to church is helpful, but being an active part of a church is imperative. This is where you will find nourishment, encouragement, and accountability.

You cannot move forward without the help of others.

The last thing I would add is this: ministering to others is time consuming. It will take energy and probably a good deal of financial investment. But we are not empowered to sit in a pew; that actually takes no empowerment at all. God empowers us, and blesses us, as we move outside ourselves with Him.

But, don't just try to serve God. Allow God to use you. Put yourself in the Way of Grace. Let your relationship with God spill over into the lives of others. Surrender yourself to God's love for others and He will love through you.

Finding a Balance

An important question at this point is, "How do you balance all these things?" There is only so much time and energy in any given day. A Christian has his own relationship with God to focus on, as well as the good of other people. Where is the balance found?

John Wesley offered this illustration,

> In a Christian believer love sits upon the throne which is erected in the inmost soul; namely, love of God and man, which fills the whole heart, and reigns without a rival. In a circle near the throne are all holy tempers; - longsuffering, gentleness, meekness, fidelity, temperance; and if any other were comprised in "the mind which was in Christ Jesus."
>
> In an exterior circle are all the works of mercy, whether to the souls or bodies of men. By these we exercise all holy tempers- by these we continually improve them, so that all these are real means of grace, although this is not commonly adverted to. Next to these are those that are usually termed works of piety - reading and hearing the word, public, family, private prayer, receiving

the Lord's supper, fasting or abstinence. Lastly, that his followers may the more effectually provoke one another to love, holy tempers, and good works, our blessed Lord has united them together in one body, the church, dispersed all over the earth- a little emblem of which, of the church universal, we have in every particular Christian congregation.[27]

For Wesley, love is the ultimate living out of the work of grace in your life. Holy love and holy tempers are the hallmark of the Christian's experience with God. He places utmost value in the love you display and the character of your life as a reflection of Jesus Himself.

But, how does love and the temperaments of the Spirit work themselves out in us?

First, in Works of Mercy, that is, ministry to others. In his illustration, he places those in the first exterior circle. Why does he put those first? Why not the Works of Piety? Why not things like prayer and meditation on scripture? Should we not be zealous first and foremost for the Church?

All these things are important, but the mind of Christ, as well as the characteristics of the Spirit, first are demonstrated in giving yourself to others. You will never be more like God than when you give. Not only that, but the process of ministry to others "continually improves" the holy tempers. God uses your ministry to others to make you more like Him. Wesley explains,

For example. Every Christian ought, undoubtedly, to be zealous for the church... For this he ought to wrestle with God in prayer; meantime using every means in his power to enlarge its borders, and to strengthen his brethren, that they may adorn the doctrine of God our Saviour.

But he should be more zealous for the ordinances of Christ than for the church itself; for prayer in public and private; for the Lord's supper, for reading, hearing, and meditating on his word; and for the much-neglected duty of fasting. These he should earnestly recommend; first, by his example; and then by advice, by argument, persuasion, and exhortation, as often as occasion offers.

Thus should he show his zeal for works of piety; but much more for works of mercy; seeing "God will have mercy and not sacrifice," that is, rather than sacrifice. Whenever, therefore, one interferes with the other, works of mercy are to be preferred. Even reading, hearing, prayer are to be omitted, or to be postponed, "at charity's almighty call;" when we are called to relieve the distress of our neighbour, whether in body or soul.[28]

Where should our focus lie? Did you hear Wesley's answer?

Whenever, therefore, one interferes with the other, works of mercy are to be preferred. Even reading, hearing, prayer are to be omitted, or to be postponed, "at charity's almighty call;" when we are called to relieve the distress of our neighbour, whether in body or soul.

As important as corporate worship is, and as vital as your own devotional life is, if something has to be laid aside, let it not be the ministry you have in the lives of others.

Therefore, loving God is first. The very fulfilling of the Law of God is dependent on this. Without the first, all the rest are meaningless anyway. Secondly, living out the character of the Spirit. But, you first practice the character of the Spirit by giving yourself to others, just as God Himself does. After that, focus on your own spiritual exercises. You can't lock yourself away with your Bible and be holy. You will have to live it out in a reflection of Jesus. And that will take giving yourself to others.

The End Result

In all you do, remember that the goal is a transformed life. Personal discipline without transformation is hard. To force yourself to be something you're not lends itself to legalism and disappointment. You will have to do things to seem holy, but you will always be disappointed in your lack of holiness.

The means of grace as a life's work interacts with the grace of God in order that you be made (or more correctly, remade) into something He has designed.

> *Do not be conformed to this age, but be transformed by the renewing of your mind, so that you may discern what is the good, pleasing, and perfect will of God.*[29]

In all you do, remember that the goal is a transformed life.

God made us in His image; His grace can let that image shine once again. But God is not asking you to fix yourself or act like something else. He is inviting you into a relationship that will change you.

The word "transformed" in Romans 12:2 is passive. It doesn't say "transform yourself." It says, "Be transformed."

Let God transform you. Your part is in meeting Him in the place He has designed for you in your transformation.

Breathe it in. Let the grace of God enter into who you are. Make prayer, scripture, and worship integral to your life.

Breathe it out. Respond to Him. Let praise, prayer, and love flow from you as naturally as your own breath.

And share it with others. Make ministering to others a consistent and natural part of who you are.

When you've mastered this, you will have just begun to live out an intentional, intimate relationship with the living God.

Breathe.

APPENDIX

Learning to Breathe

Questions for Group Study

Chapter 1: The Great Privilege

Shared life is the basis of the very nature of God.

Before anything was created—in eternity past when God simply was—He was shared life. The Father was begetting the Son, as the Spirit communicated the very substance of the Father in a relationship of life and love.

1. What difference does it make that God is a relationship of life and love rather than a single person, alone?

   ... we were created to reflect the Son—the Son begotten by the love of the Father through the Spirit's infusion; the Son relating, loving, sharing life with the Father.

2. What does "reflecting the Son" mean in everyday life? How do we live it out?

3. What are some of the blocks to relationship with God and how have you overcome them?

   Relationship with God is not only possible, it has been provided by the love of God incarnate, the love of God in action, and the love of God infused in us by His presence through the Spirit.

4. If you were advising someone in their attempt to start a relationship with God, how would you help them to move past their own trying and begin trusting?

Chapter 2: The Need to Breathe

Just as your body has this life-giving rhythm, so your soul must also have a life-giving rhythm of its own—a spiritual respiration, if you will. Breathe in God's grace, breathe out God's grace.

1. **In what ways is relationship with God like the process of breathing?**

    God is acting on the soul. It is His action first. We don't take the first step; He does. That is grace. But that action is perceived. We feel it. We know it happens. If God acts on your soul, why wouldn't you know it?

2. **When did you first feel God act on your soul, and how did you know it?**

3. **Not all responses to God are positive. What are some of the ways people respond negatively to God's moving?**

    Starting a relationship with God is not hard; He does that. You can't impress Him, entice Him, trick Him, or somehow make Him love you more. But God in His grace moves toward you. He draws you, invites you to trust Him. He imparts His life to you and gives you His love. This is all God's work. All you do is receive it.

4. **Why is it so difficult to simply receive? Why do we still try to work for God's approval?**

    Friendships go stale. Marriages go cold. Spiritual life gets boring. The remedy? Don't get comfortable.

5. **What are five things you can do keep your relationship with God from getting comfortable?**

Chapter 3: Breathe It In

God has created us in His image and part of that includes the ability to have a spiritual connection to Him.

1. You will never be satisfied in life without a relationship with God. Do you agree or disagree? Why or why not?

2. While it is God who initiates relationship with us, we have a part to play in keeping the relationship active and intentional. Describe the part the Means of Grace have played in your life.

3. This chapter uses three Means of Grace: Prayer, Bible Study, and Worship. Which of these is hardest for you, and which is easiest? Why do you think this is true?

   Don't get me wrong—God wants to hear your heart. He wants you to come to Him with your fears and desires. But His will is perfect. His timing is right. His heart and hands are working for your best. When you believe that, you can trust Him. And when you can trust Him, you can surrender to Him

4. Describe the turning point in surrender. How could you help someone who is struggling with this? What will this change about their prayer life?

5. Prayer, Bible Study, and Worship all have something in common—a shifting perspective. How does God use these Means of Grace to transform us? How has He used them in your life specifically?

6. What part does corporate worship play in your own spiritual development? How does being an active part of a local church transform you?

Chapter 4: Breathe It Out

It takes both God's acting and our reacting to complete the process of spiritual respiration, and both must be a continual part of who we are. A life consistent in these things experiences not only the grace of God, but growth in that grace.

1. Relationship with God is not just about receiving grace; we also respond to Him. Why is response to God such an important part of your Christian walk?

2. What are some of the ways your soul responds to Him?

3. When are some distinct times when your soul responded to God's grace?

   Love happens in two distinct but related directions; some people liken it to a cross made up of both vertical and horizontal beams.

   While a vertical love toward God is foundational to Christian living, the New Testament is clear that it doesn't stop there. There is a horizontal love—a love toward others that is also a reaction to grace.

4. In what way is love toward others a reaction to God's grace at work in your life?

   Praying for others will move your interest from "self" to "serve."

5. How does praying for someone else impact your own spiritual walk? How is prayer a sanctifying work?

Chapter 5: Just Breathe

It would be unethical to tell you that once you are a Christian your life gets easier, that spiritual life comes naturally, or that spiritual warfare has now ended. On the contrary, when you entered into a relationship with God, your spiritual battles began to deepen.

1. What are some of the ways spiritual warfare occurs in the life of a Christian?

    Neglect is the great enemy of your soul.

2. What means of grace are easiest for you to neglect?

3. How does neglect affect your spiritual battles?

    Sanctification is about the grace of God transforming us "spirit, soul, and body." But sanctification does not happen in a vacuum.

    John Wesley prescribed both the means of grace and ministering to others as necessary to sanctification.

4. How has God used your daily relationship with Him in the means of grace and your reaching out to others, to transform who you are?

5. The fourfold balance of Loving, Living, Giving, and Growing, found in Wesley's idea of loving God, living out the characteristics of the Spirit, giving yourself to others, and developing your own pattern of means of grace, is about balance. If you were discipling someone who was seeking God's sanctifying work in their lives, what intentional process could you use to help walk them through it?

ENDNOTES

Introduction

1   Romans 12:1

Chapter One

1   Ephesians 2:18
2   Genesis 2:7
3   John 17:3. The Greek word *ginosko* has the sense of intimate knowledge – it is even used as a Jewish idiom for sexual intimacy.
4   Athanasius, *On the Incarnation of the Word*, chapter 1, CCEL.org
5   Revelation 4:11
6   Romans 3:23
7   He actually put the plan into place prior to our existence – see Ephesians 1:4 and 1st Peter 1:20.
8   Athanasius, *On the Incarnation of the Word*, chapter 1.
9   In verses 20-21 of John 17 Jesus prayed for believers to be one – and not just His New Testament disciples but for believers throughout the ages. "*I pray not only for these, but also for those who believe in Me through their message. May they all be one, as You, Father, are in Me and I am in You. May they also be one in Us, so the world may believe You sent Me.*"
10   John 17:1-3
11   Romans 8:14-15
12   Ephesians 2:18

Chapter Two

1   John Wesley, *The Great Privilege of Those that are Born of God*.
2   Ibid.
3   God's love for mankind is based on His love for the Son. We are created to reflect the Son and we receive as a consequence the Father's love for the Son. This love is unwavering and unchanging.
4   John 1:12
5   Romans 5:8
6   Romans 5:6-11
7   John 15:1, 4 and 6

Chapter Three

1   John Wesley, *The Means of Grace*.
2   In his sermon *On Zeal*, John Wesley laid out the means of grace fully like this: "By these we exercise all holy tempers—by these we continually improve them, so that all these are real means of grace, although this is not commonly adverted to. Next to these are those that are usually termed works of piety—reading and hearing the word, public, family, private prayer, receiving the Lord's supper, fasting or abstinence. Lastly, that his followers may the more effectually provoke one another to love, holy tempers, and good works, our blessed Lord has united them together in one body, the church, dispersed all over the earth- a little emblem of which, of the church universal, we have in every particular Christian congregation."
3   John Wesley, *The Scripture Way of Salvation*. "It is incumbent on all that are justified to be zealous of good works. And these are so necessary, that if a man willingly neglect them, he cannot reasonably expect that he shall ever be sanctified; he cannot grow in grace, in the image of God, the mind which was in Christ Jesus; nay, he cannot retain the grace he has received; he cannot continue in faith, or in the favour of God. What is the inference we must draw herefrom, Why, that both repentance, rightly understood, and the practice of all good works,—works of piety, as well as works of mercy (now properly so called, since they spring from faith), are, in some sense, necessary to sanctification."
4   Chris Lohrstorfer, *Surrendered: A forty day devotional based on the*

Lenten Prayer of St. Ephrem. (Teleios Press, Jackson, MS, 2017)

5   Romans 8:26-27
6   Psalm 77:11-12
7   Luke 22:41
8   This is a good reason why you should start prayer in worship; it sets the stage for surrender by arranging your perspective of God properly.
9   John Wesley, *The Means of Grace.*
10   2nd Timothy 2:15
11   Proverbs 27:17
12   1 Corinthians 11:28
13   Ephesians 5:19-21
14   Hebrews 10:23-25

Chapter Four

1   John Wesley, *The Great Privilege of those who are Born of God.*
2   Ibid.
3   1 John 4:19
4   Evangelism often involves helping others see what God is doing in their life.
5   John 13:34-35
6   Romans 5:5
7   "'But what good works are those, the practice of which you affirm to be necessary to sanctification?' First, all works of piety; such as public prayer, family prayer, and praying in our closet; receiving the supper of the Lord; searching the Scriptures, by hearing, reading, meditating; and using such a measure of fasting or abstinence as our bodily health allows. Secondly, all works of mercy; whether they relate to the bodies or souls of men; such as feeding the hungry, clothing the naked, entertaining the stranger, visiting those that are in prison, or sick, or variously afflicted; such as the endeavouring to instruct the ignorant, to awaken the stupid sinner, to quicken the lukewarm, to confirm the wavering, to comfort the feeble-minded, to succour the tempted, or contribute in any manner to the saving of souls from death. This is the repentance, and these the 'fruits meet for repentance,' which are necessary to full sanctification. This

is the way wherein God hath appointed His children to wait for complete salvation." Wesley, John, *The Scripture Way of Salvation*.

8   Ibid.

9   Philippians 2:3-4

Chapter Five

1   Revelation 2:2-3

2   Revelation 2:4

3   Thomas Aquinas (1225-1274)

4   Hebrews 3:12-13

5   1st John 3:9

6   Hebrews 3:12-14

7   John Wesley, *The Great Privilege of those that are born of God*

8   Matthew 14:22-33

9   John 15:4-6. "Remain in Me, and I in you. Just as a branch is unable to produce fruit by itself unless it remains on the vine, so neither can you unless you remain in Me. I am the vine; you are the branches. The one who remains in Me and I in him produces much fruit, because you can do nothing without Me. If anyone does not remain in Me, he is thrown aside like a branch and he withers. They gather them, throw them into the fire, and they are burned."

10   Ibid.

11   Hebrews 2:1

12   Hebrews 3:12

13   Hebrews 4:1

14   Hebrews 4:11

15   Hebrews 6:11-12

16   John Wesley, *Letter to John Trembath*, August 17, 1760.

17   Ibid.

18   Ibid.

19   John Wesley, *The Means of Grace*.

20   John Wesley, *On Visiting the Sick*.

21   Technically, only faith is required for any work of grace. However, what is faith? Is it mere belief? Saving faith moves beyond belief to application of the belief. Repentance, both in initial salvation and sanctification is in some sense a prerequisite for faith.

22   John Wesley, *The Scripture Way of Salvation.*

23   1st Thessalonians 5:23

24   I believe there is psychological work as much as a spiritual work that has to be done in confronting yourself. In order to be open to God you have to be open to yourself first.

25   John Wesley, *The Repentance of Believers.*

26   John Wesley, *The Scripture Way of Salvation.*

27   John Wesley, *On Zeal.*

28   Ibid.

29   Romans 12:2

Made in the USA
Monee, IL
23 July 2021

73719566R00056